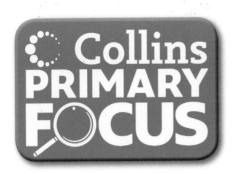

# Grammar and Punctuation
## Pupil Book 2

## Louis Fidge

William Collins' dream of knowledge for all began with the publication of his first book in 1819. A self-educated mill worker, he not only enriched millions of lives, but also founded a flourishing publishing house. Today, staying true to this spirit, Collins books are packed with inspiration, innovation and practical expertise. They place you at the centre of a world of possibility and give you exactly what you need to explore it.

Collins. Freedom to teach.

Published by Collins
An imprint of HarperCollins*Publishers* Ltd.
77–85 Fulham Palace Road
Hammersmith
London
W6 8JB

**Browse the complete Collins catalogue at**
**www.collinseducation.com**

Text © Louis Fidge and Sarah Lindsay 2011
Design and illustrations © HarperCollins*Publishers* 2011

Previously published as *Collins Primary Grammar and Punctuation*, first published 1997; and *Collins Focus on Grammar and Punctuation*, first published 2002.

10 9 8 7 6 5 4 3

ISBN: 978-0-00-741072-9

Louis Fidge and Sarah Lindsay assert the moral right to be identified as the authors of this work.

British Library Cataloguing in Publication Data
A Catalogue record for this publication is available from the British Library.

Cover template: Laing and Carroll
Cover illustration: Julian Mosedale
Series design: Neil Adams and Garry Lambert
Copy editor: Jean Rustean
Illustrations: Shirley Chiang, Bridget Dowty, Rob Englebright, Steve Evans, Kevin Hopgood, Bethan Matthews, Andrew Midgley, Martin Remphry, James Walmesley, Gwyneth Williamson, Jakki Wood

Printed and bound by Printing Express Limited, Hong Kong.

**MIX**
Paper from
responsible sources

FSC™
www.fsc.org   **FSC˚ C007454**

FSC™ is a non-profit international organisation established to promote the responsible management of the world's forests. Products carrying the FSC label are independently certified to assure consumers that they come from forests that are managed to meet the social, economic and ecological needs of present and future generations, and other controlled sources.

Find out more about HarperCollins and the environment at
**www.harpercollins.co.uk/green**

# Contents

# Parts of speech

**Grammar** is the study of the way we use words to make sentences. Words can be divided into groups called **parts of speech**. Three **parts of speech** are **adjectives**, **nouns** and **verbs**.

The **powerful eagle lands.**

An **adjective** is a **describing** word. **Adjectives** tell us more about nouns.

A **noun** is a **naming** word. A **noun** can be the **name** of a person, place or thing.

Most **verbs** are words that describe actions. This **verb** tells us what **is happening**.

## Getting started

**Copy these sentences.**
**Choose a verb from the box to fill each gap.**

| catches | shouts | carries | crawls | plants | chases | sail | types |

1. The old turtle _____ up the hill.
2. The porter _____ the suitcases to our hotel room.
3. Mr Blake _____ some seeds in his garden.
4. The secretary _____ lots of letters.
5. Emma _____ at the top of her voice.
6. We _____ our boat out to sea.
7. The bull _____ the children across the field.
8. The eagle _____ the animal in its claws.

## Now try these

1.  **Think of a noun to go with each adjective.**

    a) a red _____           b) the brown _____

    c) some golden _____     d) an empty _____

    e) a soft _____          f) the warm _____

    g) some tall _____       h) a foolish _____

2.  **Now write four sentences of your own, using your answers from Question 1.**

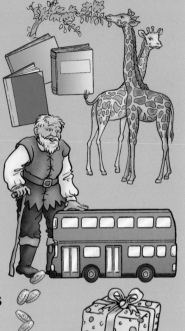

3.  **Think of an adjective to go with each noun.**

    a) a _____ parcel        b) the _____ sea

    c) some _____ children   d) a _____ wind

    e) a _____ accident      f) some _____ trees

    g) an _____ giant        h) the _____ books

4.  **Now write four sentences of your own, using your answers from Question 3.**

## Practise your punctuation ., '?! " "

Punctuation marks make writing easier to understand.

1.  **Punctuate these sentences correctly.**
    **Put in the capital letters, full stops, commas and question marks.**

    a) the frightened child approached the dark castle

    b) what made that funny noise

    c) the small boy was carrying a big bag
       a book a pointed stick and an apple

    d) the old door creaked and opened

    e) a strange old lady stood in the shadows

2.  **Now underline the verbs, circle the nouns and cross out the adjectives.**

# Unit 2 — Nouns (common and proper)

A **noun** is the **name** of a person, place or thing.

**Common** (or ordinary) **nouns** are the **names** of general people, places or things.

A **common noun** starts with a **small letter**.

The **boy** went by **train** from the **station**.

A **proper noun** is the **name** of a **particular** person, place or thing.

A **proper noun** starts with a **capital letter**.

**Tom** went by **Eurostar** from **London**.

## Getting started

Copy this table.
Write each noun from the box in the correct column.

| Proper nouns | Common nouns |
|---|---|
| Snow White | crocodile |

> Snow White   crocodile   bus   Fluff   Nigeria   letter
> Mr Barnes   house   shop   River Nile   The Times   day   Mars
> pet   Sunday   word   woman   Easter   Nasir   sentence

# Now try these

1. Copy these sentences.
   Underline the proper nouns. Circle the common nouns.
   The first one has been done to help you.
   a) The (coach) to Birmingham was full.
   b) At Diwali some people have a party.
   c) The boat sailed down the River Jordan.
   d) During his holiday Ben visited Portugal.
   e) Sir Francis Drake was a famous explorer.
   f) My favourite football team is Chelsea.
   g) Mrs Rossetti is a keen gardener.
   h) The book was The Pink Pyjamas by Barbara Miller.

2. Complete this alphabetical list of people and places.
   Don't worry if you can't think of a name or place for every letter.

   Andrew lives in America.

   Billy lives in Bermuda.

   Claire lives in Canada.

# Practise your punctuation

1. Punctuate these sentences correctly.
   a) ann moore lives in edinburgh
   b) my address is 14 king street
   c) have you ever been to germany canada mexico or jamaica
   d) the mountaineer climbed mount everest
   e) is christmas in november or december

2. Now underline the proper nouns and circle the common nouns.

# Verbs

Most **verbs** are words that describe **actions**.
They tell us what someone is **doing** or what is **happening**.
Some **verbs** are **being** words.

The frog **hops** into the water.

↑

This is an **action verb**.
It tells us what the frog is **doing**.

The frog **is** green and brown.

↑

This is a **being verb**.
It tells us what the frog **is**.

## Getting started

1. **Copy these sentences.**
   **Underline the action verb in each one.**
   a) Tadpoles nibble weeds.          b) Tadpoles swish their tails.
   c) The frog jumped on to a rock.   d) The frog croaked loudly.

2. **Choose a being verb from the box to fill each gap.**

   | am | are | is | was | were | will be |
   |---|---|---|---|---|---|

   a) Tadpoles _____ baby frogs.
   b) I _____ too hot.
   c) Victoria _____ Queen of Great Britain.
   d) Ali _____ good at spelling.
   e) Tomorrow we _____ one day older.
   f) The Egyptians _____ inventive people.

# Now try these

1. **Copy these sentences.**
   **Choose the correct action verb to fill each gap.**

   a) If you _____ the ball I will _____ it. (catch, throw)

   b) Cork _____ on water but metal _____. (floats, sinks)

   c) The woman _____ a hole and then _____ it in again.
   (filled, dug)

   d) A captain _____ and the team _____. (leads, follows)

   e) The child _____ the heavy weight and then _____ it.
   (dropped, lifted)

   f) A customer _____ things but a shopkeeper _____ them.
   (buys, sells)

2. **Copy these sentences.**
   **Underline the being verb in each one.**

   a) The shopping bag is full.

   b) The doctor was late.

   c) Tomorrow will be Sunday.

   d) The Vikings were good fighters.

   e) How are you today?

   f) I am tired.

# Practise your punctuation

1. **Punctuate the sentences in this story correctly.**

   sooty looked up at the table hungrily
   the budgerigar was in its cage on
   the table the cat jumped up the bird
   was frightened mrs sharp heard all
   the noise and ran into the room
   she was very angry with the cat

2. **Now underline the action verbs and circle the being verbs.**

# Sentences and phrases

A **sentence** is a group of words that **makes sense** on its own.
Every **sentence** must contain a **verb**.
A **phrase** is a group of words that **does not make sense** on its own.
Most **phrases** are **short**. Most **phrases do not** contain **verbs**.

The girls ran along the beach.

This is a **sentence**.
It **makes sense** on its own.
It contains a **verb**.

along the beach

This is a **phrase**. It **does not make sense** on its own.
It **does not** contain a verb.

## Getting started

1. **Copy this table.**
   **Write the sentences and phrases in the correct columns.**

| Sentences | Phrases |
| --- | --- |
|  |  |

a) A ghostly sea captain spoke to the girl.
b) the silver fish
c) The ship sank into the sea.
d) The dog chewed the bone.
e) this morning
f) top of the rock
g) King Henry was fond of sport.
h) The Sun came out.
i) Stand up.
j) The girl ran out of the cave.

2. **Now underline the verb in each sentence.**

## Now try these

1. **Choose a phrase from the box to complete each sentence.**

> in its cage     because of the fog     through the town
>
> over the wall     at night     after the rain

a) The zoo keeper put the vulture back _____.

b) The soil was very wet _____.

c) Three girls climbed _____.

d) Owls come out to hunt _____.

e) The fire spread _____.

f) The football match had to be cancelled _____.

2. **Write six of your own sentences using each phrase from the box.**

> under the sea     down the hill     at midnight
>
> outside the house     in the woods     because of the cold

## Practise your punctuation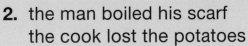

Write these pairs of sentences adding the missing punctuation and swapping the verbs so that each sentence makes sense. The first one has been done to help you.

1. the lady laid an egg
   the hen fried an egg

   *The lady fried an egg.*
   *The hen laid an egg.*

2. the man boiled his scarf
   the cook lost the potatoes

3. fishes trot
   horses swim

4. the goat sang the grass
   the girl ate the song

5. the builder shaved the house
   the man built his chin

6. the teacher roasted her husband
   the doctor kissed a chicken

# Adjectives (1)

An **adjective** is a **describing** word.

**Adjectives** give us more information about **nouns**.

**Adjectives** make sentences **more interesting**.

The dragon came out of the cave.

We can improve this sentence by adding some **adjectives**.

The **fearsome, fiery** dragon came out of the **huge, dark** cave.

## Getting started

**Choose the best adjective to fill each gap.**

1. The _____ beggar wore _____ clothes. (poor, bright, dirty, new)
2. The _____ giant lives in an _____ castle. (ugly, cold, old, blue)
3. The _____ girl ate a _____ apple. (purple, little, juicy, hairy)
4. The _____ lady smiled as she sat on the _____ bench.
   (wooden, cheerful, red, rubber)
5. The _____ cat chased the _____ mouse. (fat, dry, noisy, tiny)
6. The _____ monster had a _____ nose.
   (wobbly, long, strange, metal)
7. The _____ clown tripped over his _____ boots.
   (funny, thin, heavy, big)
8. A _____ hedgehog walked up the _____ path.
   (narrow, high, prickly, quiet)

## Now try these

1. **Copy these sentences.**
   **Leave out the adjectives.**
   **The first one has been done to help you.**

   a) The brave knight fought the fiery dragon.

   ### The knight fought the dragon.

   b) The mighty wind ripped up the old tree.

   c) Some green racing cars sped along the wide track.

   d) Where have the gigantic dinosaurs gone?

   e) The small, wooden boat was tossed about by the rough sea.

   f) A strange little man with a pointed hat sang a sad song.

2. **Copy these sentences.**
   **Put in some adjectives to make the sentences more interesting.**
   **The first one has been done to help you.**

   a) The dog ate the bone. *The hairy dog ate the enormous bone.*

   b) The boy climbed the tree.

   c) A burglar forced the door open.

   d) The girl went out on her bike.

   e) The house was in the woods.

## Practise your punctuation

Punctuate the sentences in this story correctly.
Each time you come to the adjective *nice*, replace it
with a more interesting word.

saturday was a nice day youssef dressed in some
nice clothes he called for alice she lived in a nice house
they went for a nice walk in the park youssef bought
a nice drink alice bought a nice ball they played on
the swings and had a nice time

# Subjects and verbs

Every **sentence** has a **verb**. Every **sentence** also has a **subject**.
The **subject** is the **main person or thing** in the **sentence**.

Scott saw an elf.

This is the **subject** of the **sentence**.
The **subject** is usually found in front
of the **verb**.

This is the **verb**.
It tells us what Scott **did**.

## Getting started

**Copy these sentences.**
**Underline the subject and circle the verb in each one.**
**The first one has been done to help you.**

1. <u>Sandra</u> (saw) a fairy.
2. Dogs bark.
3. Tortoises eat lettuce.
4. The helicopter crashed.
5. Eddie followed the strange troll.
6. Charlie found some gold.
7. The snake slid through the grass.
8. Sam won the race.
9. Curry is my favourite dinner.
10. Jack and Jill went up the hill.

## Now try these

1. **Think of a subject to complete each sentence.**
   **Then underline the verb in each sentence.**

   a) _____ is a good friend.

   b) _____ swing through the trees.

   c) _____ hunt for food at night.

   d) _____ has lovely handwriting.

   e) _____ buried the treasure.

   f) _____ scared the children.

2. **Think of a sentence ending to go with each subject.**
   **Then underline the verb in each sentence.**

   a) The proud princess …

   b) The submarine …

   c) Humpty Dumpty …

   d) A roaring dragon …

   e) Some old people …

   f) The strong wind …

## Practise your punctuation    .,'?!""

1. **Match these subjects and sentence endings.**
   **Write the sentences with the correct punctuation.**

   | Subjects | Sentence endings |
   | --- | --- |
   | a) penguins | give us milk cheese butter and cream |
   | b) the pop star | has very sharp teeth |
   | c) a shark | are black and white and live in the antarctic |
   | d) the space monster | had a pointed head and green teeth |
   | e) cows | sang a pop song to the crowd |

2. **Now underline the verbs and circle the subjects.**

# Nouns (singular and plural)

We can write **nouns** in the **singular** or the **plural**.
**Singular** means just **one**.
**Plural** means **more than one**.

one rattle    two rattles         one baby       two babies

We just add **s** to many **singular nouns** to make them **plural**.

When a **noun** ends in a **consonant** + **y** we change the **y** to **i** and add **es**.

Take care when you change the **subject** of a sentence into a **plural**.
The **subject** of the sentence and the **verb** must always agree.

The **baby is** asleep.     The **babies are** asleep.

## Getting started

**Copy and complete this table.**

| Singular | Plural |
|----------|--------|
| school   |        |
| fly      |        |
|          | cars   |
| city     |        |
| picture  |        |
|          | lorries |
| lady     |        |

# Now try these

1. **Copy these sentences.**
   **Change the subject of each sentence into the plural.**
   **Change the verb to agree with the subject.**
   a) The fly is on the table.
   b) The door was open.
   c) The story is boring.
   d) The lorry was speeding.
   e) The dog is barking loudly.
   f) The factory has lots of windows.

2. **Copy these sentences.**
   **Change the subject of each sentence into the singular.**
   **Change the verb to agree with the subject.**
   a) The pictures are well painted.
   b) The families were sitting on the beach.
   c) The walls were very dirty.
   d) The ponies are galloping round the field.
   e) The cars are moving on to the ferry.
   f) The cities are full of heavy traffic.

# Practise your punctuation

1. **Write these sentences correctly.**
   **Change the verb in each sentence to agree with the subject.**
   **Remember to add the missing capital letters and punctuation.**
   a) the pennies was in the purse
   b) some tigers is roaming through the trees
   c) a horse were eating a carrot
   d) the baby were drinking a bottle of milk
   e) lorries cars ships and aeroplanes is all means of transport
   f) ponies has manes

2. **Now underline all the plural nouns in each sentence.**

# Exclamation marks

An **exclamation mark** is a punctuation mark.

This is an **exclamation mark**: !

An **exclamation mark** comes at the **end of a sentence**.
It shows that the writer feels **strongly** about something.

! can show **excitement** or **surprise**.

! can give **warning**.

! can show that someone is **hurt**.

! can show that something happens **suddenly**.

## Getting started

Here are some exclamations and some questions.
Make a list of the exclamations and then a list of the questions.
Add the missing punctuation mark to finish each sentence.

1. Come here quickly
2. How do they do that
3. I feel quite dizzy
4. Smash Bang Crash
5. What is the time
6. Where are you going
7. Look what I have found
8. Help I'm stuck
9. Why are you sad
10. When can we go home

# Now try these

Write what you think each person is saying.
Remember to finish each sentence with an exclamation mark.

# Practise your punctuation

Punctuate these sentences correctly.

1. is it safe to open the door now
2. do not do that
3. come here
4. what do you think you are doing
5. hands up this is a robbery
6. what is for tea
7. that is a nasty cut
8. help I am trapped in the mud

# Verbs (past and present tenses)

> **Verbs** written in the **present tense** tell us what is happening **now**.
>
> **Verbs** written in the **past tense** tell us what happened **in the past**.

Today Tom **rows** his boat.

This **verb** is in the **present tense**.
It tells us what is happening **now**.

Last week Tom **rowed** his boat.

This **verb** is in the **past tense**.
It tells us what happened **in the past**.
Verbs in the **past tense** often have **ed** at the end.

## Getting started

**Copy these sentences.**
**Underline the verb in each one.**
**Write whether it is in the present tense or the past tense.**
**The first one has been done to help you.**

1. Ben <u>finishes</u> his homework. *present tense*
2. Rosie helps her mum.
3. Joe looked at a good book yesterday.
4. The mouse squeaked loudly.
5. On Saturday we walked to the shops.
6. The boy smiles at his friend.
7. On holiday I visited France.
8. The log floated down the river.
9. Emma sits in the sun.
10. The frog jumped on to the rock.

## Now try these

1. Write a pair of sentences using each verb from the box.
   In the first sentence, the verb should be in the present tense.
   In the second sentence, the verb should be in the past tense.
   The first one has been done to help you.

| jump | shout | talk | help | float |
| play | listen | watch | laugh | act |

Today Sam jumps. → Yesterday Sam jumped.

2. Copy and complete this table.
   Take care. Some of the verbs in the past tense do not follow the rules!

| Verb | Present tense | Past tense |
|------|---------------|------------|
| wait | Tom waits | |
| skip | | Tom skipped |
| cook | Tom cooks | |
| hop | Tom hops | |
| eat | | Tom ate |

## Practise your punctuation

1. Punctuate these sentences correctly.
   a) the children climb a tree
   b) beth sucks her thumb
   c) andy and dan play in the park
   d) the dog chases the postman
   e) i eat an apple

2. Underline the verb in each sentence.

3. Write each sentence again, changing the verb into the past tense.

# Adverbs

An **adverb** is a word that gives **more meaning** to a **verb**.
Many **adverbs** tell us **how** something happened.

The sun shone **brightly**.

This is an **adverb**.
It tells us **how** the sun shone.

Many **adverbs of manner**
(how adverbs) end in **ly**.

## Getting started

1. **Copy these sentences.**
   **Underline the adverb in each one.**
   a) The rain fell heavily.   b) The river flowed rapidly.
   c) The boy spoke rudely.    d) Shahla was dressed smartly.
   e) The time passed slowly.  f)  Cross the road safely.
   g) The girl sang loudly.    h) The nurse treated me gently.

2. **Choose an adverb from the box to fill each gap.**
   **You can only use each adverb once.**

   | carefully | quietly | crossly | soundly | noisily | quickly |

   a) I eat crisps _____.
   b) I listen _____.
   c) I sleep _____.
   d) I whisper _____.
   e) I run _____.
   f)  I argue _____.

## Now try these

1. **Form an adverb from each adjective.**
   **The first one in each group has been done to help you.**
   **Look carefully at how the spellings of the words change in each group when *ly* is added.**

   a) deep → **deeply**   b) light   c) proud   d) clever
   e) glad   f) fierce   g) clear   h) slow

   i) humble → **humbly**   j) noble   k) gentle   l) simple
   m) feeble   n) horrible   o) sensible   p) terrible

   q) happy → **happily**   r) angry   s) heavy   t) hungry
   u) lucky   v) merry   w) easy   x) lazy

2. **Copy and complete each adverb web.**

   a)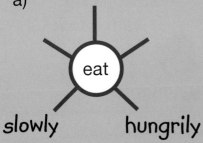
   slowly   hungrily

   b)

   c)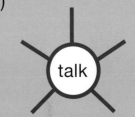

## Practise your punctuation

1. **Punctuate the sentences in this story correctly.**

   the children were throwing things running shouting and laughing what a noise mrs turner walked quickly down the corridor she stormed angrily into the room the noise stopped suddenly the children slowly returned to their seats and got on quietly with their work

2. **Now underline all the adverbs.**

# Progress Unit A

1.  **Copy these sentences.**
    **Underline the subject and circle the verb in each one.**

    a) My brother plays loud music.

    b) Joanne acts very well.

    c) I am sailing my boat this morning.

    d) The passengers board the bus.

2.  **Now write the sentences in the past tense.**
    **The first one has been done to help you.**

    a) My brother played loud music.

3.  **Write a sentence including each of these phrases.**

    a) on the dinosaur    b) in the water    c) last night

    d) when the dragon    e) after a time    f) with a fork

4.  **Copy this table.**
    **Write the nouns from the box in the correct columns.**

| Common nouns | Proper nouns |
|---|---|
|  |  |

> bird    Coronation Street    house    Mrs Finch    February
> day    Jupiter    holiday    Fernbank Junior School    Holland
> Diwali    mother    snow    Joanne    envelope    King John

5.  **Copy these sentences.**
    **Think of an adverb to fill each gap.**

    a) Mark behaved very _____.

    b) The crowd shouted _____.

    c) Last night the rain fell very _____.

    d) The elephant lumbered _____ along.

## 6. Copy and complete this table.

| Singular | Plural |
|----------|--------|
| sock | |
| shirt | |
| fly | |
| story | |
| dog | |
| baby | |
| boat | |
| swimmer | |
| army | |
| city | |

## 7. Choose an adjective from the box to make each sentence more interesting.

> playful    tall    crowded    stormy    serious    bright

a) The puppy in the park was very _____.

b) The car and the lorry were involved in a _____ accident.

c) The _____ trees in the forest made it seem very dark.

d) Tom was blinded by the _____ sunlight.

e) The _____ weather made the ferry crossing very unpleasant.

f) It was difficult to move because the streets were so _____.

## 8. Copy these sentences.
### Underline the being verbs.
### Circle the action verbs.

a) Alvin Moonburst is a pop star who sings very well.

b) The Romans were good soldiers who fought bravely.

c) Dogs bark loudly but they are good pets.

d) The doctor came when I was unwell.

e) I am a good speller and score full marks in tests.

f) Bananas are my favourite fruit and I eat lots of them.

# Pronouns

A **pronoun** is a word that **takes the place of** a **noun**.

Sam knew that **Sam** was different from the other geese.

Sam knew that **he** was different from the other geese.

In this sentence we use the pronoun **he** instead of the noun **Sam**.

This stops us from **repeating the noun**, making the sentence **sound better**.

## Getting started

Copy these sentences.
**Choose a pronoun from any of the boxes to fill each gap.**

1. The children were sad when _____ were told off.

2. Rachel said that _____ was fed up.

3. Do _____ like chips? Yes, _____ do!

4. "Pass the ball to _____!" Tom shouted.

5. Katie asked Harry to give _____ a sweet.

6. When Dan got home _____ watched television.

7. Where is the ball? _____ is under the chair.

8. "Come with _____, _____ are going shopping," the girls said.

9. The birds flew away when the cat chased _____.

10. Dan smiled at Mum. _____ smiled back at _____.

| he, him | it | you | I, me | they, them | we, us | she, her |

# Now try these

Copy these sentences.
Replace the underlined words with a pronoun.
The first one has been done to help you.

1. Pick up your book and put your book on the desk.

   *Pick up your book and put it on the desk.*

2. My sister and I are going on holiday because my sister and I like camping.

3. Ben knew exactly what to do when Ben saw the lost child.

4. When the girl walked in the rain the girl got wet.

5. Gran gave Tom a hug because Gran loved Tom.

6. The race was very important. The race turned out to be very exciting.

7. After the woman had read the book the woman returned the book to the library.

8. Ann and I spent the night at a hotel. Ann and I left the next morning.

# Practise your punctuation

1. **Punctuate these sentences correctly.**
   **There may be more than one sentence in each answer.**

   a) we live in a big house with a large garage i keep a bike a sledge a go-kart and some footballs in it

   b) pull the rope hard if you let it go the post will fall over

   c) the television programme bored me it was very dull

   d) we went to the match mr smart gave us a lift

   e) joe asked mrs crown the way to the shop she told him how to get there

   f) give me an apple please

2. **Now underline all the pronouns.**

# Main clauses

A **main clause** is a **group of words** that can be used as
a **whole sentence**.
A **clause** contains a **subject** and a **predicate**.

Every **simple sentence** can be divided into **two parts**:
a **subject** and a **predicate**.

The chicken ↑     laid an egg. ↑

This is the **subject** of
the sentence. The subject is
the **main thing** or **person**.

This is the **predicate**. The **predicate**
is **the rest of the sentence**.
It always contains a **verb** which tells us
what is happening.

## Getting started

Match the subjects and predicates to make sentences.
The first one has been done to help you.

| Subjects | Predicates |
|---|---|
| **1.** The snake | bake bread. |
| **2.** A grey cat | was chewing a bone. |
| **3.** Bakers | chugged out of the harbour. |
| **4.** Comedians | hid in Sherwood Forest. |
| **5.** Robin Hood | slithered through the grass. |
| **6.** My pet dog | jumped over our fence. |
| **7.** Some fishing boats | tell jokes. |

1. *The snake slithered through the grass.*

# Now try these

1. **Copy these sentences.**
   **Circle the subjects and underline the predicates.**
   **The first one has been done to help you.**

   a) (My youngest brother) eats a lot of pizzas.

   b) The big black crow flew into the clear blue sky.

   c) A fierce wild dog snarled at the frightened boy.

   d) Three strong men pushed the car back on to the road.

   e) Some straggly sheep were grazing in the field.

   f) Kieran and Jayesh ran into the cave.

   g) The new dentist inspected my teeth.

   h) The teacher in the playground blew the whistle.

   i) A small fishing boat was battered by the huge waves.

   j) The metal robot moved with strange clanking sounds.

2. **Now tick the verb in each sentence.**

# Practise your punctuation

1. **Punctuate these sentences correctly.**

   a) the young tiger pounced on sara

   b) the rescue dog found the injured
      explorer on top of the icy mountain

   c) the police officer chased the young burglar

   d) a red sports car crashed into the back of the coach

   e) the dragon ate prince rupert for breakfast

   f) the wise old wizard turned tess into a toad

2. **Write the sentences again, changing the subject in each one.**
   **The first one has been done to help you.**

   a) Sara pounced on the young tiger.

# Adjectives (2)

An **adjective** is a **describing** word.
**Adjectives** tell us more about **nouns**.
**Adjectives** make writing **more interesting**.

There were **three** cars.

**Numbers** are often used as **adjectives**.

The **second** car was an estate car.

**Adjectives** can tell us the **order** of nouns.

Joe liked the **red** car best.

**Adjectives** can add **colour**.

He was very **excited** when he bought it.

**Adjectives** can describe **feelings**.

## Getting started

**Copy these sentences.**
**Think of a colour, number or order adjective to fill each gap.**

1. I bought a bunch of _____ bananas.
2. I won first prize and Billy won the _____ prize.
3. Calum bought a bag of _____ cherries.
4. It takes _____ people to argue.
5. In autumn, _____ leaves fall from the trees.
6. The swan was as _____ as snow.
7. Sophie's skirt was as _____ as grass.
8. There are _____ players in a football team.

# Now try these

1. **Think of an ending for each of these sentences.**
   **Then underline the feeling adjective in each sentence.**

   a) I felt angry when …

   b) Ali felt excited when …

   c) Jane was jealous when …

   d) At school I was pleased when …

   e) He felt brave because …

   f) The small boy was lonely when …

   g) Mrs Smith was worried because …

   h) The swimmer was surprised when …

   i) I would feel shy if …

   j) The cat was curious when …

2. **Choose the adjective which you think describes the strongest feeling in each pair.**

   a) pleased or delighted

   b) ecstatic or happy

   c) interested or fascinated

   d) gloomy or miserable

   e) annoyed or furious

   f) terrified or scared

# Practise your punctuation .,'?!""

1. **Punctuate these sentences correctly.**

   a) have you ever felt lazy have you ever wanted to stay in bed all day

   b) dan felt happy he felt contented satisfied pleased and delighted all at the same time

   c) edward threw the ball at sue unfortunately it missed and hit the window crash mr clark appeared at the door looking very angry

   d) it was shireens ninth birthday she had invited four friends to her party sam nazma dan and dean all came

2. **Now underline all the adjectives in each sentence.**

# Prepositions

A **preposition** is a word that tells us the **position** of one thing in relation to another.

These words are **prepositions**.

The alien had two curly horns **on** its head.
**Between** its eyes it had a pointed nose.
It had a large mouth with sharp teeth **under** its nose.

## Getting started

**Copy these sentences.**
**Choose a preposition from the box to fill each gap.**

| into | between | behind | in | on | above | beside | under |

1. The green alien is _____ the spacecraft.
2. The red alien is _____ the ladder.
3. The orange alien is climbing _____ the spacecraft.
4. The blue alien is _____ the spacecraft.
5. The yellow alien is _____ the spacecraft and the rock.
6. The purple alien is _____ the rock.
7. The pink alien is _____ the rock.
8. The brown alien is flying _____ the rock.

# Now try these

**Think of a preposition to complete each sentence.**

1. Tara received a lovely present _____ her aunt.
2. John draped his coat _____ a chair.
3. The pirate gold was buried _____ the ground.
4. Mrs West turned off the light _____ her bed.
5. The dog chased _____ the cat at great speed.
6. Jamal ran _____ the race track twice.
7. The robber threw the stone _____ the shop window.
8. The car crashed _____ the traffic lights.
9. The lottery money was divided _____ two winners.
10. The magician pulled a rabbit _____ his hat.

# Practise your punctuation

1. **Match the beginning and ending of each sentence.**
   **Write the sentences with the correct punctuation.**

   a) in march the farmer put a fence          off his horse

   b) jenny and jake sailed their boat          through the woods

   c) the jockey fell          round his field

   d) our dog smudge ran          into the icy water

   e) the swimmer dived          across the road

   f) on sunday ben walked his dog          down the river

2. **Now underline the preposition in each sentence.**

An **adjective** is a **describing** word.

When we compare **two** nouns we use a **comparative** adjective.

When we compare **three or more** nouns we use a **superlative** adjective.

The Moon is **big.** ⟵ This is an **adjective**.

The Earth is **bigger.** ⟵ This is a **comparative adjective**. Many comparative adjectives end in **er**.

The Sun is the **biggest.** ⟵ This is a **superlative adjective**. Many superlative adjectives end in **est**.

# Getting started

**Copy and complete this table.**

| Adjective | Comparative adjective | Superlative adjective |
|---|---|---|
|  | smaller | smallest |
| new | newer |  |
| slow |  | slowest |
|  | faster |  |
|  |  | wildest |
| hard |  |  |
|  |  | longest |
| soft |  |  |
|  |  | sharpest |

## Now try these

1. Write the comparative and superlative forms of each adjective. The first one in each group has been done to help you.

   a) wise → wiser → wisest

   b) brave  c) safe  d) strange  e) tame  f) white  g) large

   h) hot → hotter → hottest

   i) big  j) red  k) sad  l) wet  m) thin  n) slim

   o) busy → busier → busiest

   p) heavy  q) noisy  r) lucky  s) pretty  t) happy  u) dry

2. Copy these sentences. Choose the correct comparative or superlative adjective to fill each gap.

   a) A rhinoceros is fat. A hippo is _____ but an elephant is _____ .

   b) Ann is hungry. Kim is _____ but Sam is _____ .

   c) My rabbit is tame. My cat is _____ but my dog is _____ .

## Practise your punctuation  .,'?!""

1. Punctuate these sentences correctly.

   a) gorillas live in africa they are taller stronger fiercer and heavier than humans

   b) the three aliens approached the red one was hairy and the blue one was hairier still but the purple one was the hairiest thing i have ever seen

2. Now underline the comparative adjectives and circle the superlative adjectives.

# Prefixes

Opposites are words whose meanings are as **different** as possible from each other.

We can sometimes give a verb the opposite meaning by adding a **prefix** like **un** or **dis** to the beginning of the verb.

The bus driver **loaded** the luggage.

The bus driver **unloaded** the luggage.

These verbs have **opposite** meanings.

## Getting started

1. **Write the opposite of each verb by adding the prefix *un*. The first one has been done to help you.**

   a) wrap  **unwrap**      b) pack          c) dress

   d) do                    e) tie           f) cover

   g) buckle                h) bolt          i) fold

2. **Copy these sentences, changing each verb to give the opposite meaning.**

   a) Maria packed her case on Saturday.

   b) Ahmed soon got dressed.

   c) The knight buckled his belt.

   d) The old lady unbolted the door.

   e) Sue unwrapped the present carefully.

## Now try these

1. Write the opposite of each verb by adding the prefix *dis*.
   The first one has been done to help you.
   a) trust  *distrust*      b) agree           c) like
   d) obey                   e) connect         f)  please
   g) appear                 h) allow           i)  arm

2. Copy these sentences, changing each verb to give
   the opposite meaning.
   a) Suddenly, as if by magic, the fluffy white rabbit appeared.
   b) The football players all agreed with the referee.
   c) I really like sprouts.
   d) The plumber called to connect the water supply.
   e) Dogs always obey their owners!
   f)  Tom knew just how to displease his teacher.
   g) The referee disallowed the goal.
   h) The bandits were soon disarmed.
   i)  The rider distrusted the horse.

## Practise your punctuation

1. Punctuate these sentences correctly.
   a) mr barnes filled the watering can
   b) joe abdul mark and sophia arrived on friday
   c) when did you sell that lovely picture
   d) mrs simons lost her purse in the grass
   e) the children whispered to each other
   f)  the soldiers captured some spies

2. Underline the verb in each sentence.

3. Write each sentence again, changing the verb to give
   the opposite meaning. This time you will need to change the verb
   completely instead of adding a prefix.

# Apostrophes (possession)

An **apostrophe** is a punctuation mark. This is an apostrophe: '

An **apostrophe** is used to show who **owns** something.

If the owner is **singular**, **'s** is added, even if the word ends in **s**.

Brian**'s** story was very good.

Jess**'s** story was even better.

When the owner is **plural**, **'s** is added but if the word ends in **s only the apostrophe** is added.

The children**'s** stories were all very good.

The boys**'** stories were the best.

## Getting started

**Who owns each item?**
**Add the missing singular nouns to fill each gap.**
**The first one has been done to help you.**

1. the <u>dog's</u> ball

2. the _____ hat

3. the _____ food

4. the _____ book

5. the _____ bandage

6. the _____ boots

7. the _____ hay

8. the _____ game

9. the _____ pond

## Now try these

1. **Add the missing plural nouns to fill each gap.**
   **Be careful! Some will only need an apostrophe.**
   **The first one has been done to help you.**

   a) the field belonging to the sheep      the _sheep's_ field

   b) the pencils belonging to children      the _____ pencils

   c) the food belonging to the animals      the _____ food

   d) the clothes belonging to the girls      the _____ clothes

   e) the flowers belonging to the patients      the _____ flowers

   f) the cars belonging to the policemen      the _____ cars

2. **Apostrophes are used incorrectly in these phrases.**
   **Write them correctly.**

     a) the teachers' book    b) the children' game    c) the boy's pens

## Practise your punctuation   .,'?!"" 

**Write these sentences using apostrophes correctly.**
**Put in the capital letters and full stops.**

1. sams knee hurt

2. jamess bike was stolen

3. the foxes den is comfortable and dry

4. mum looked for nazars dirty washing

5. the wind broke lailas new tent

6. the ladies clothes were hanging up

A **comma** is a **punctuation mark**. This is a comma:  **,**
**Commas** show us where to take a slight **pause**.
**Commas** help us to understand the **meaning** of a sentence.

In the cold, dark, silent depths of the sea, the shark lies in waiting.

The shark, with its black back and white stomach, has a terrible bite.

## Getting started

1. **Punctuate these phrases with commas.**
   a) a nasty mean spiteful ogre
   b) neat careful tidy writing
   c) hot bright sunny days
   d) some cold clear sparkling water
   e) a cool shady leafy forest

2. **Copy these sentences.**
   **Put in a comma where the reader needs to pause.**
   **Reading the sentences aloud might help.**
   a) The Pyramids which are in Egypt are enormous.
   b) Barney who came last was very upset.
   c) Mr Younnas our next-door neighbour is very nice.
   d) However hard she tried Wendy could not catch any fish.
   e) We arrived in Paris the capital of France.
   f) Jane my sister is good at singing.

## Now try these

Punctuate these sentences correctly.
Think carefully about where to put the commas.

1. dogs don't wear glasses do they
2. what's the matter johnny
3. oh dear the lift is stuck
4. half an hour later sophie came out of the cinema
5. please sir can you help me
6. if you turn left you will soon come to the park
7. hello mr salim it's very hot isn't it
8. in a cave on the far side of the mountain there lived a dragon
9. louise who was only nine easily won the race
10. st george brave and valiant saved the maiden

## Practise your punctuation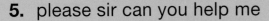

Add the missing punctuation to the sentences in this story.
Don't forget the missing commas.

the children cold and frightened walked quickly across the moor suddenly they came across a small flint hut with a candle burning in the window the children though needing shelter felt nervous about knocking who would come to the door

# Progress Unit B

1. **Complete each of these sentences with a colour, order or number adjective.**

a) There are _____ cars.

b) The fourth car is _____.

c) The _____ car is green.

d) The first car is _____.

e) The yellow car is _____.

f) The fifth car is _____.

2. **Copy these phrases and underline the preposition in each one.**

a) playing in the park

b) sitting on a chair

c) running through the woods

d) flying over the sea

e) swimming under the water

f) standing by a tree

g) stopping outside a shop

h) going up the stairs

3. **Copy each pair of sentences.**
   **Choose a pronoun from the box to replace the underlined words.**
   **You can use each pronoun more than once.**

| them | it | him | they | she | her |
|------|-----|------|-------|------|------|

a) The boy could not carry the box.
   The box was too heavy for the boy.

b) Mrs Bryant bought a new car.
   Mrs Bryant paid a lot for the new car.

c) The firefighters fought the fire.
   The firefighters took a long time to put the fire out.

d) Hannah keeps goldfish. Hannah feeds the goldfish every day.

e) Sam and Ben have a dog called Sally.
   Sam and Ben take Sally for walks.

**4. Copy these sentences.**
**Circle the subjects and underline the predicates.**

a) My sister can stand on her head.

b) Our classroom has thirty desks.

c) The sun shone brightly all day.

d) The flag was very colourful.

e) Several horses galloped around the field.

f) The big brown dog is barking furiously.

g) Youssef wrote a good story.

h) The noisy children were playing football.

**5. Copy and complete this table.**

| Adjective | Comparative adjective | Superlative adjective |
|---|---|---|
| old | | |
| long | | |
| wet | | |
| big | | |
| large | | |
| nasty | | |

**6. Copy these sentences and add the missing commas.**

a) The River Thames a very long river flows through London.

b) Visit Australia the land of opportunity.

c) The cat unaware of the dog wandered into the back garden.

**7. Add the missing possessive nouns to fill each gap.**
**Don't forget to put the apostrophe in the right place.**

a) the chicks belonging to the hens      the _____ chicks

b) the foals belonging to the ponies      the _____ foals

c) the puppies belonging to the dog      the _____ puppies

d) the lamb belonging to the sheep      the _____ lamb

**8.** Write three short paragraphs describing your day yesterday.

**Paragraph 1:** the morning

**Paragraph 2:** the afternoon

**Paragraph 3:** the end of the day

**9.** Add *dis* or *un* to the beginning of each verb to give it the opposite meaning.

a) obey          b) screw          c) lock

d) approve       e) appear         f) coil

g) load          h) own            i) do

**10.** Match the beginning and ending of each sentence. Write the sentences correctly.

a) A phrase — is the main person or thing in the sentence.

b) Every sentence — is used to compare two nouns.

c) The subject — is a small group of words that does not make sense on its own.

d) We use a plural — gives more meaning to a verb.

e) The present tense of a verb — takes the place of a noun.

f) An adverb — when we are talking about more than one thing.

g) A pronoun — tells us what is happening now.

h) A comparative adjective — must contain a verb.